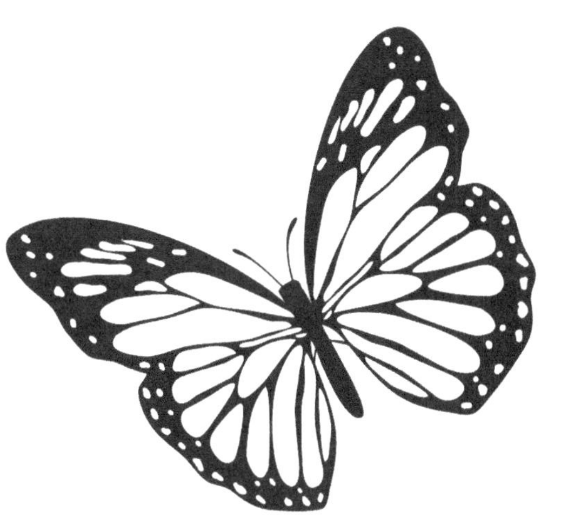

This Book Belongs to:

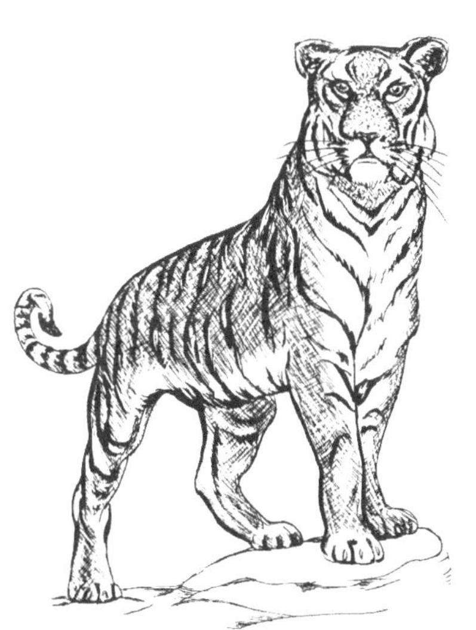

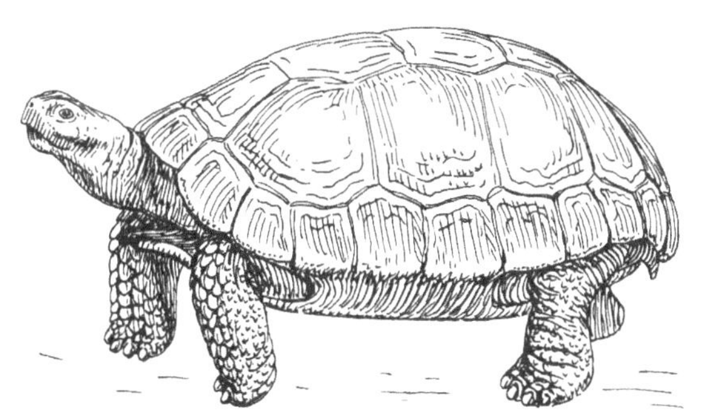

Dear Reader,

It is with great joy that we present to you "**Coloring the Wild World: Color Adventures for Little Ones**". This book has been created with immense care and dedication, aiming to provide moments of fun and learning for children.

We are deeply grateful that you have chosen our book to be a part of your little one's creative journey. Each page has been designed to inspire, educate, and most importantly, entertain.

We hope this book becomes a source of joy and discovery for you and your child, and that the colors you choose to fill these pages bring unforgettable moments of creativity and togetherness.

With gratitude,

Emerson Carvalho

Test Cölör page

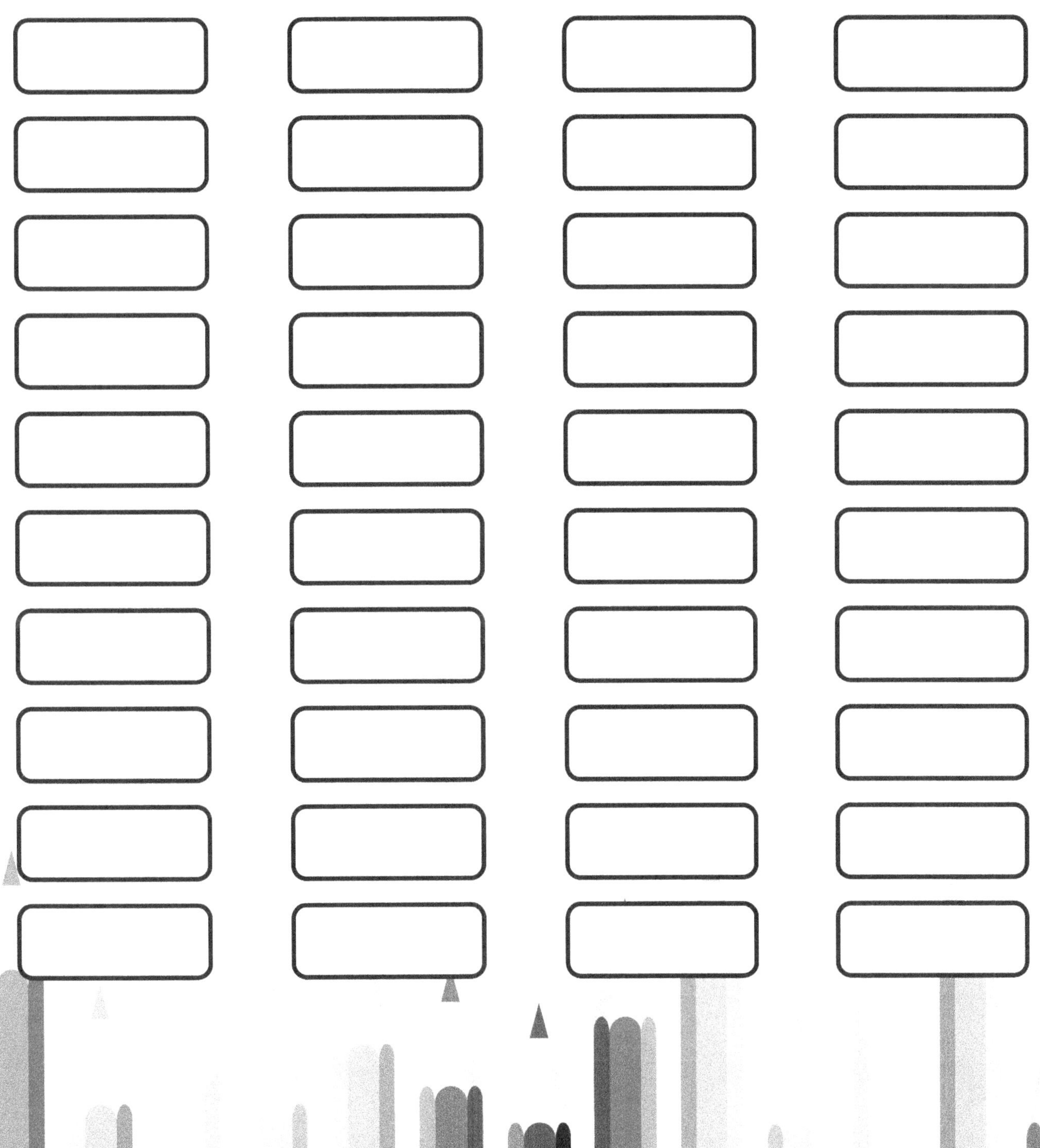

KOALA

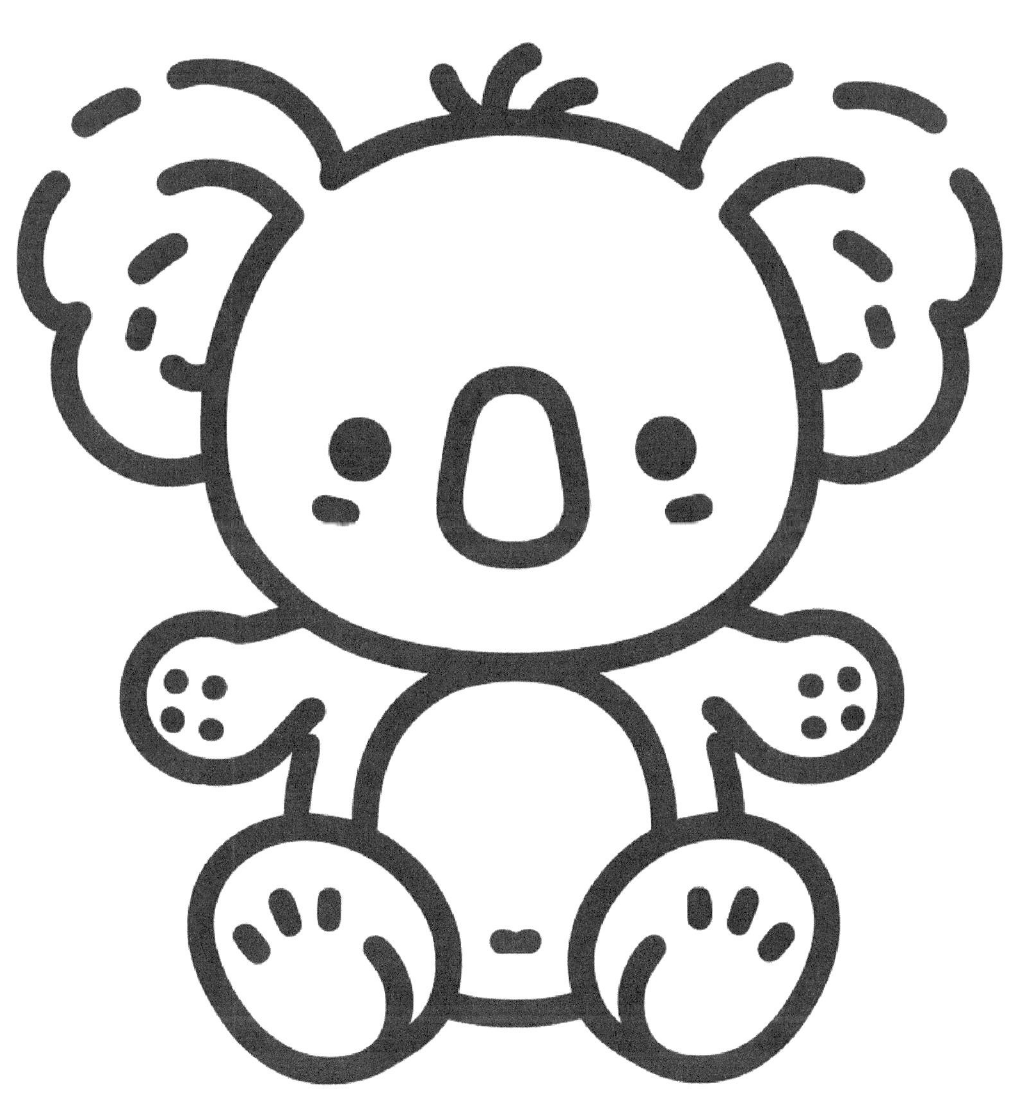

TOUCAN

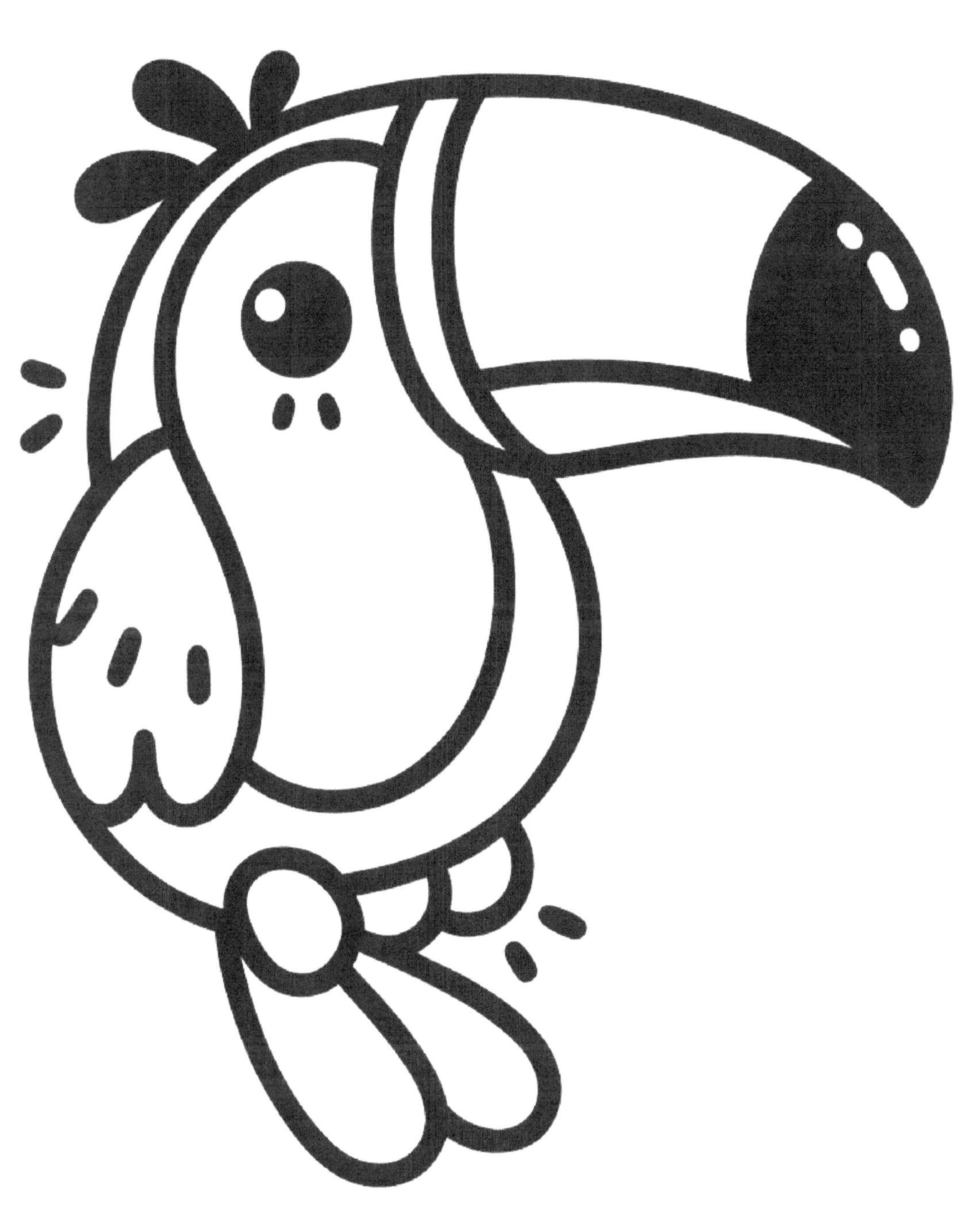

PANDA

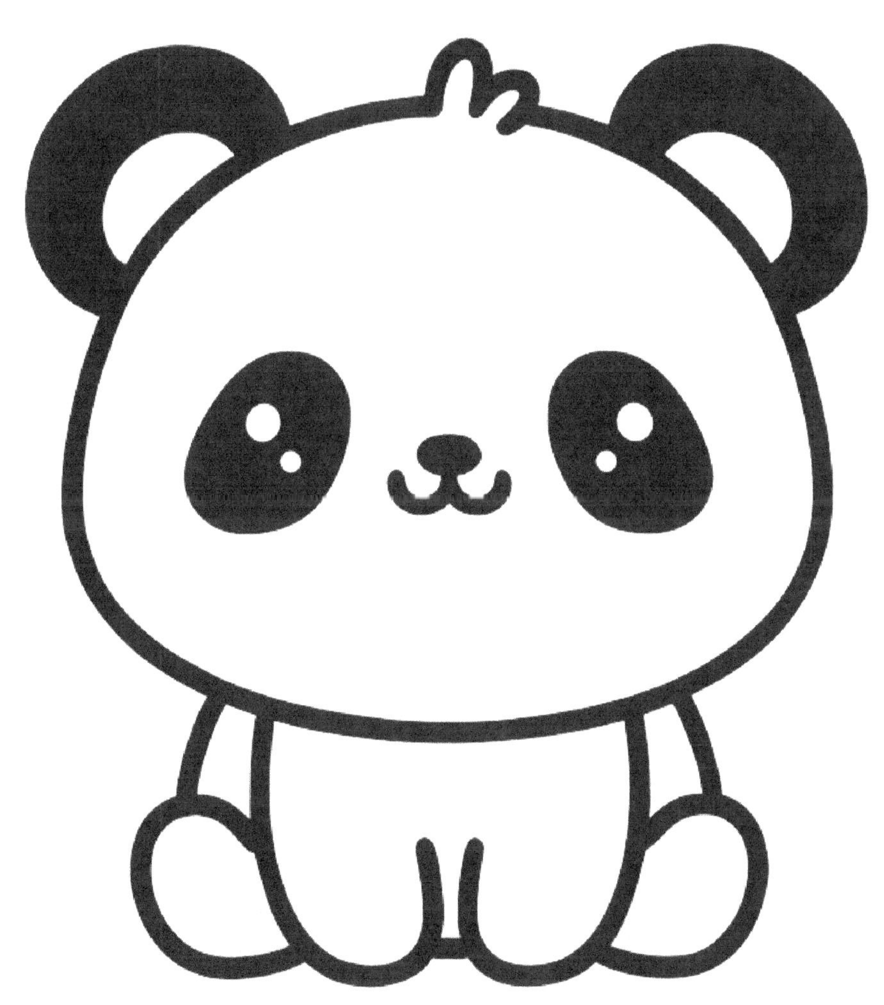

LION

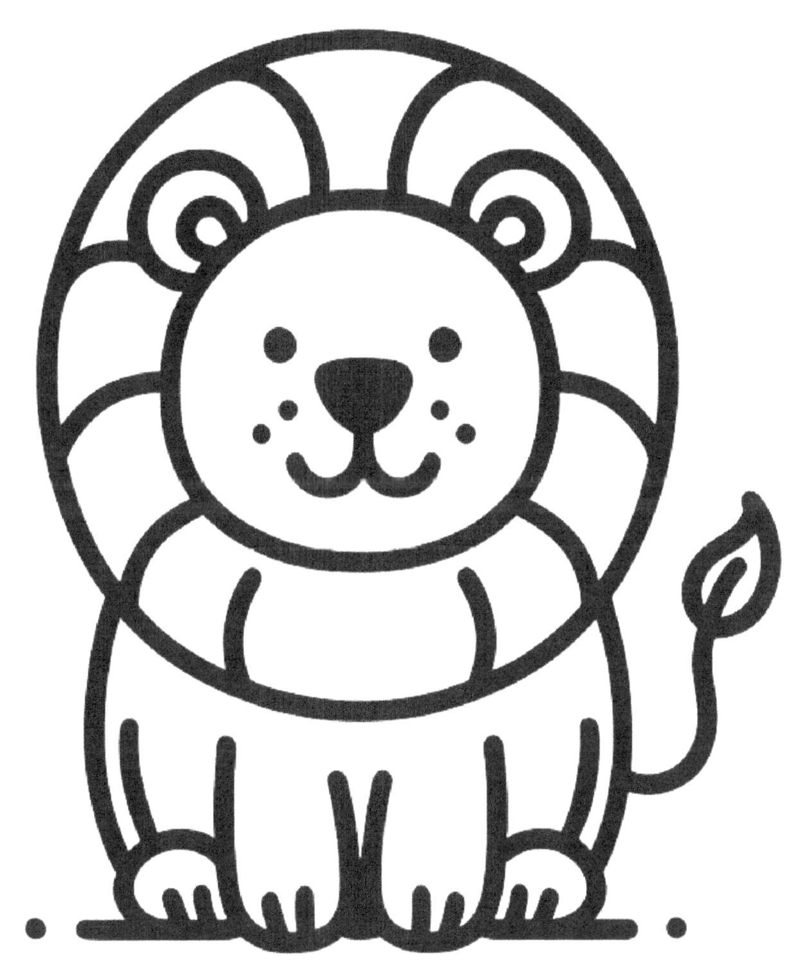

ELEPHANT

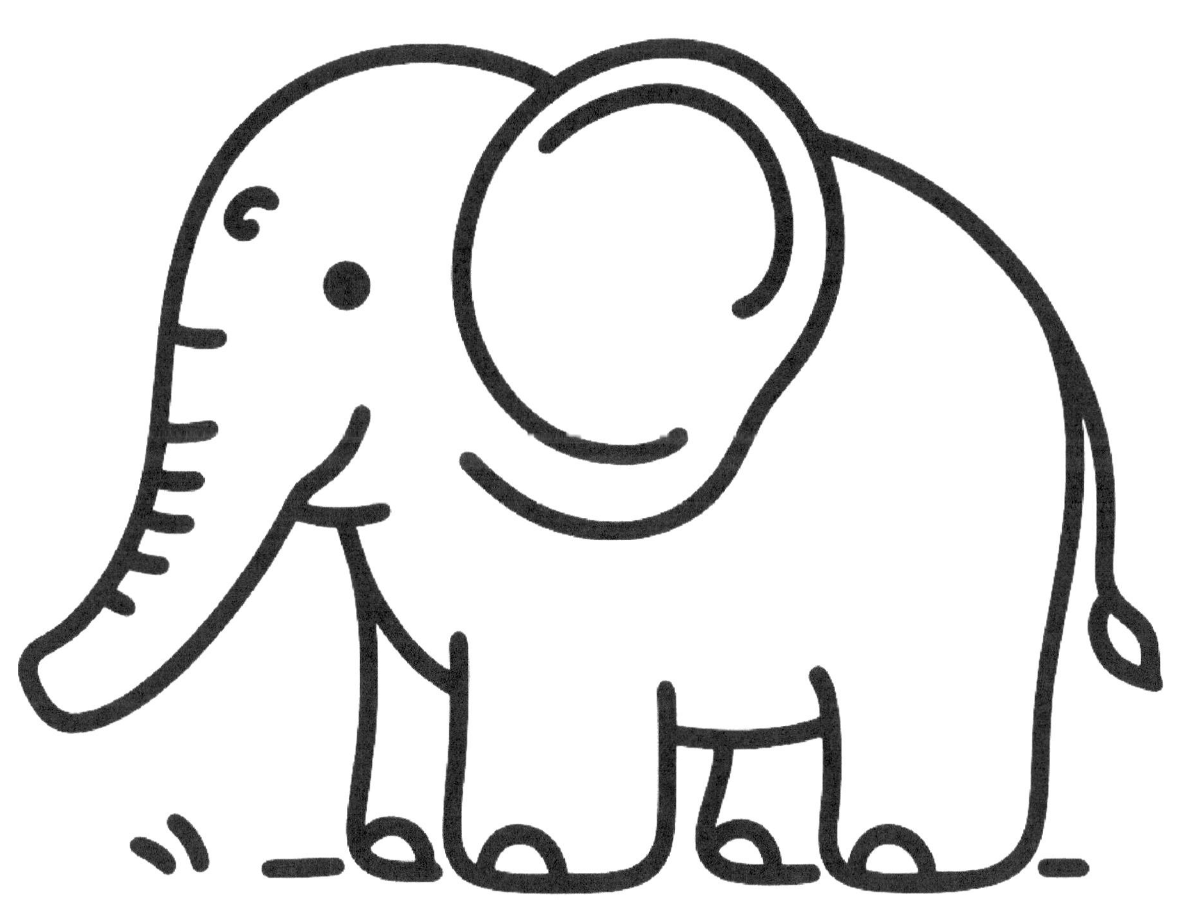

FISH

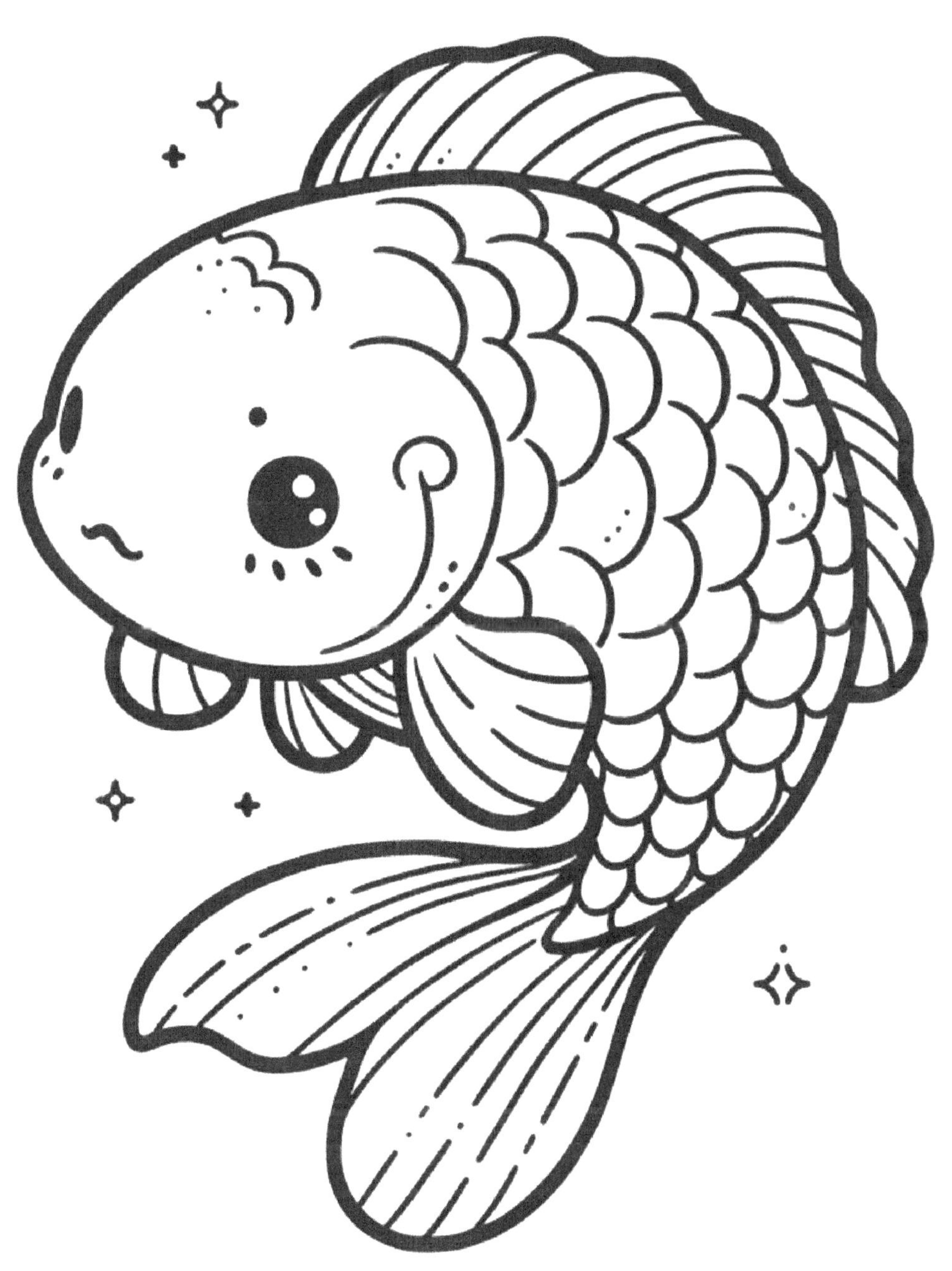

BEAR

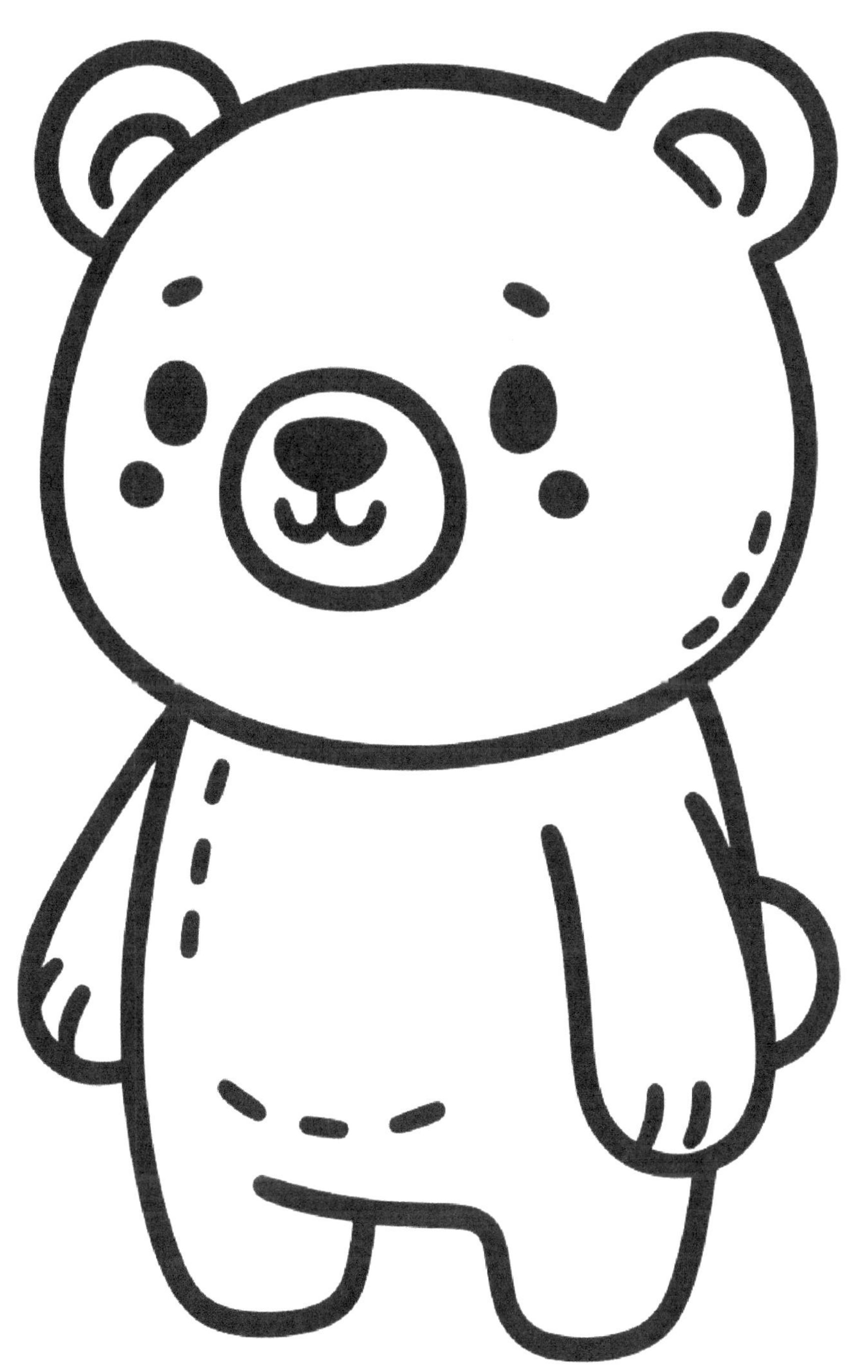

PENGUIN

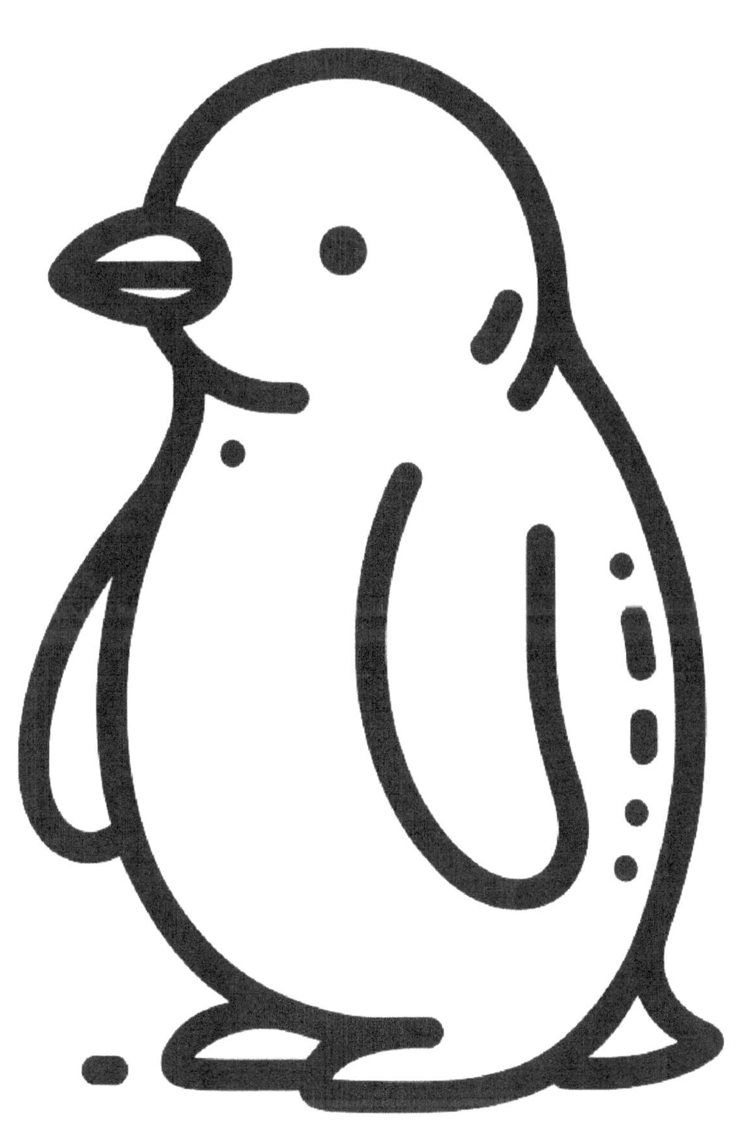

Moose

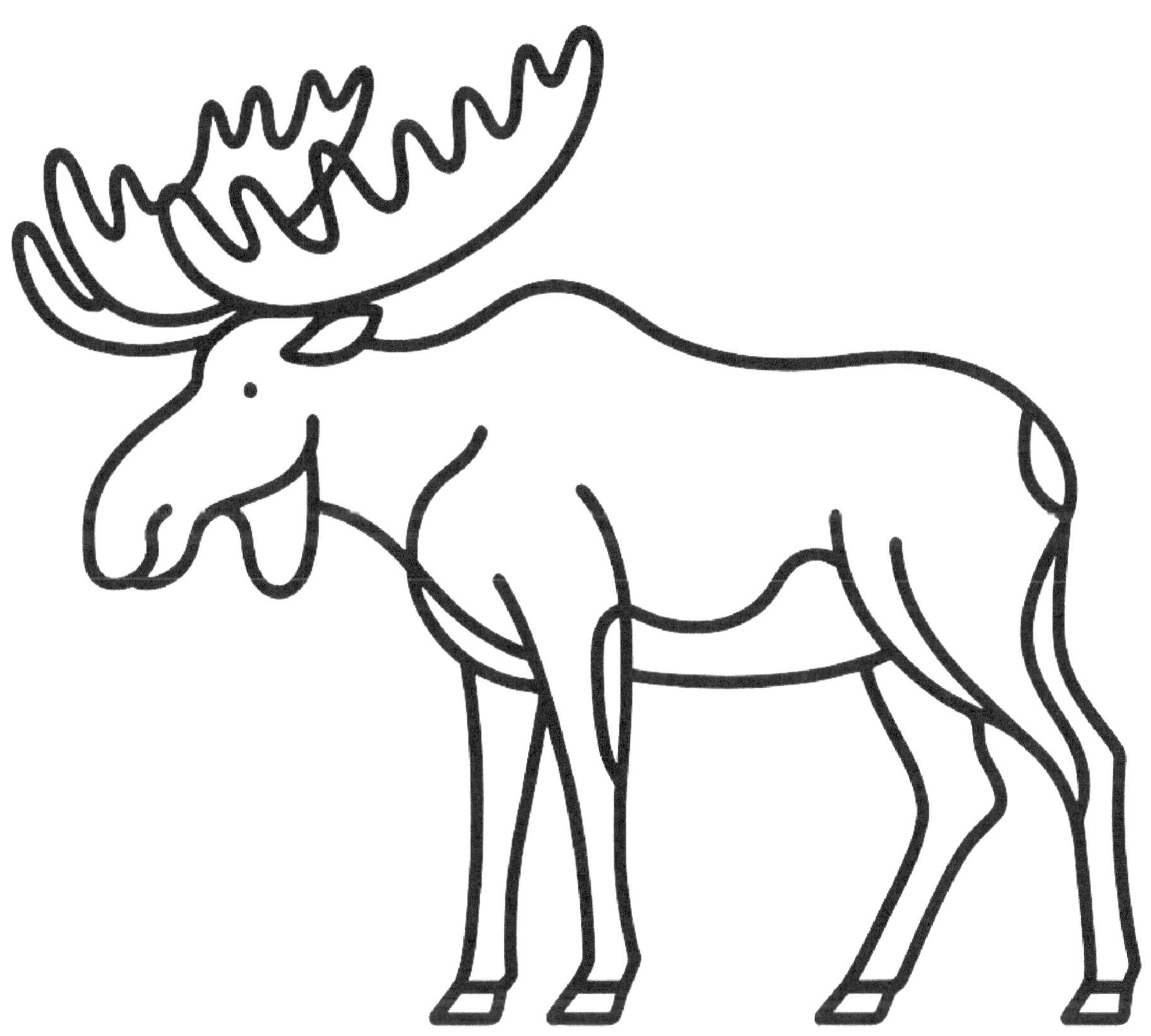

FLAMINGO

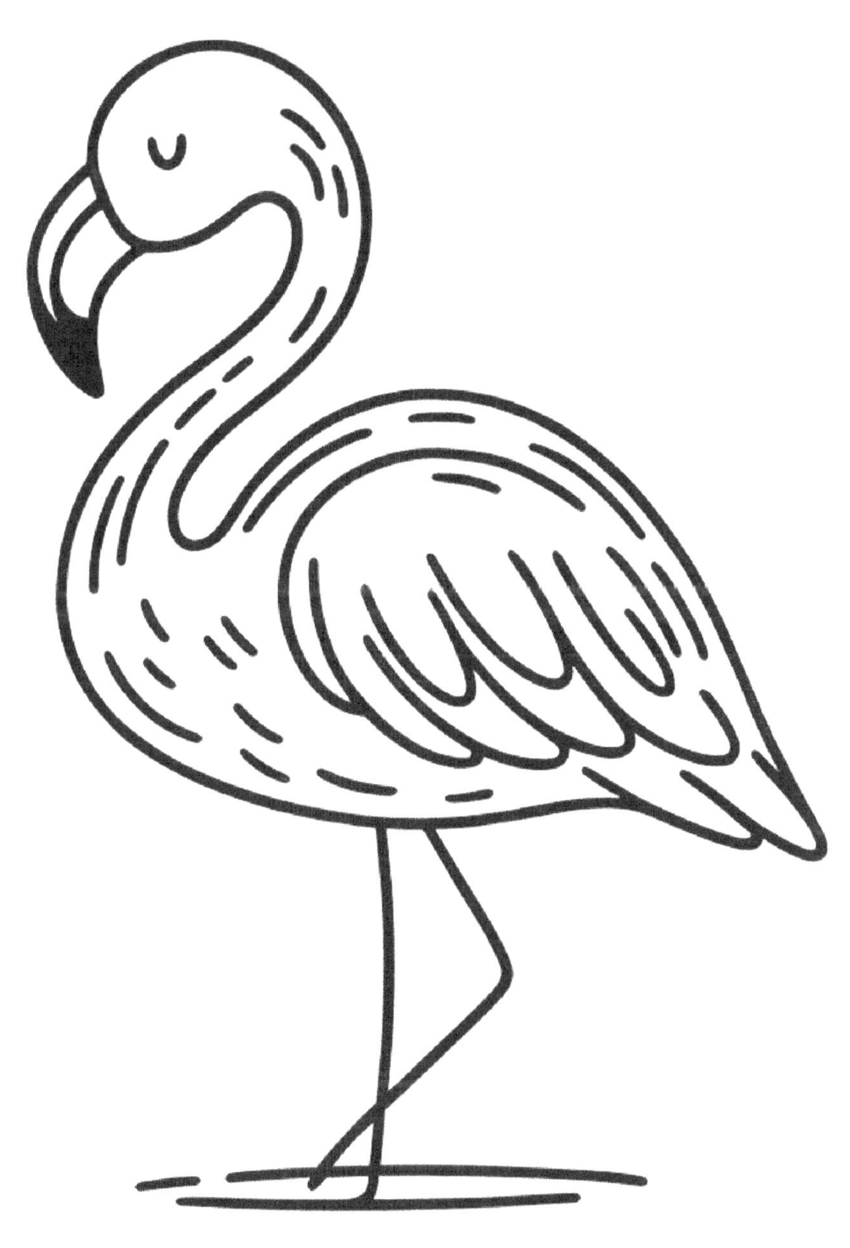

TIGER

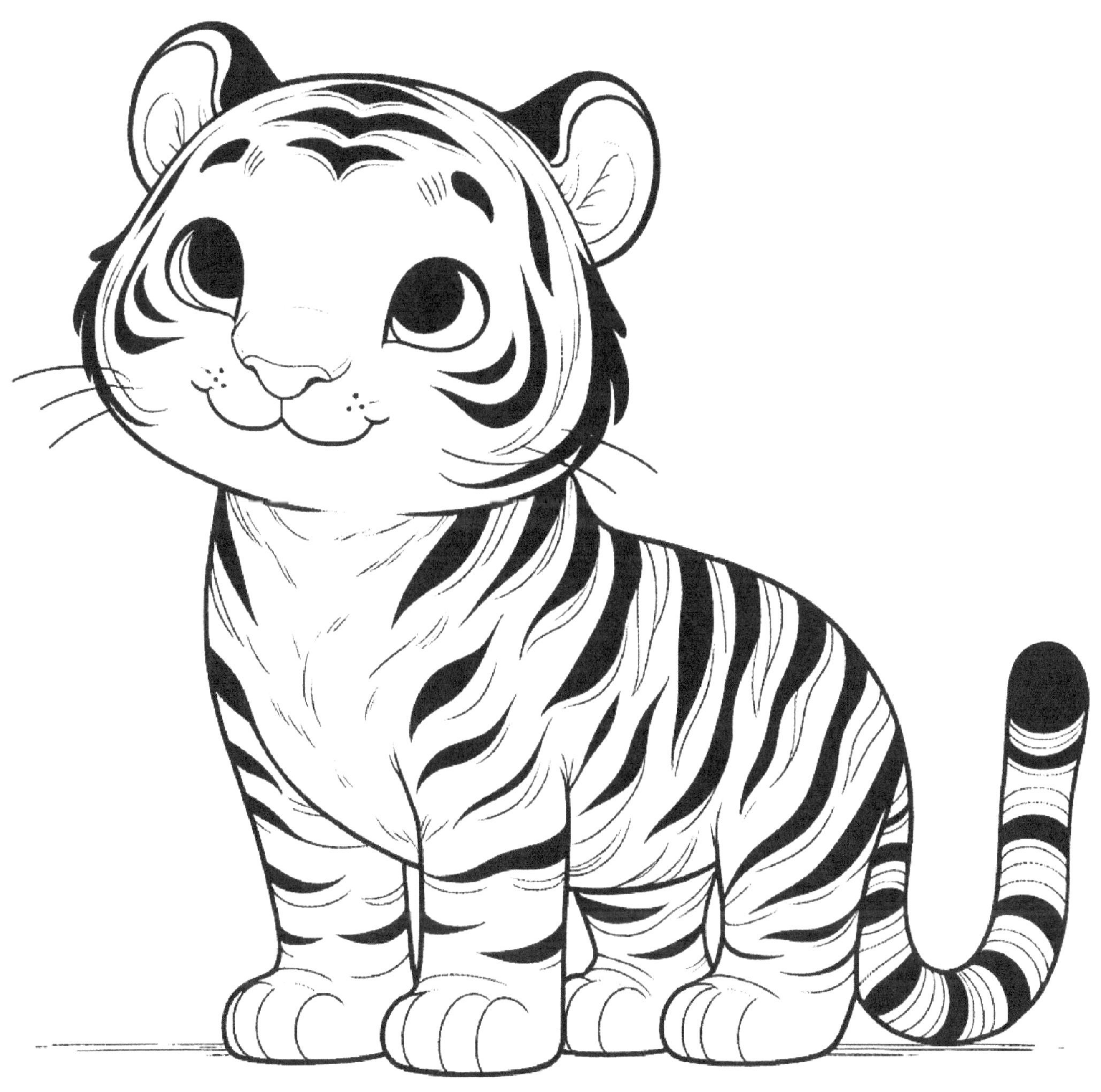

SQUIRREL

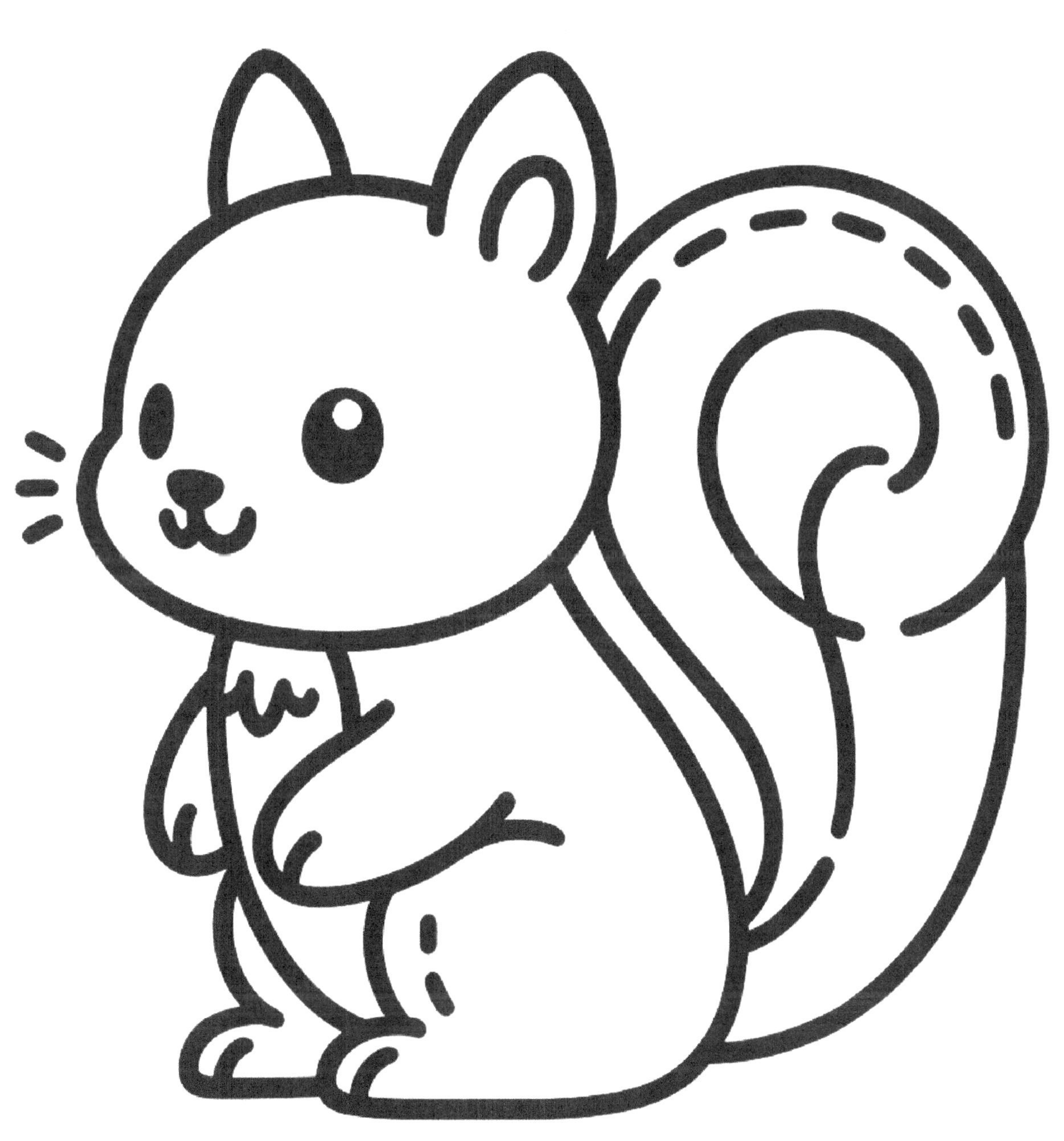

DOLPHIN

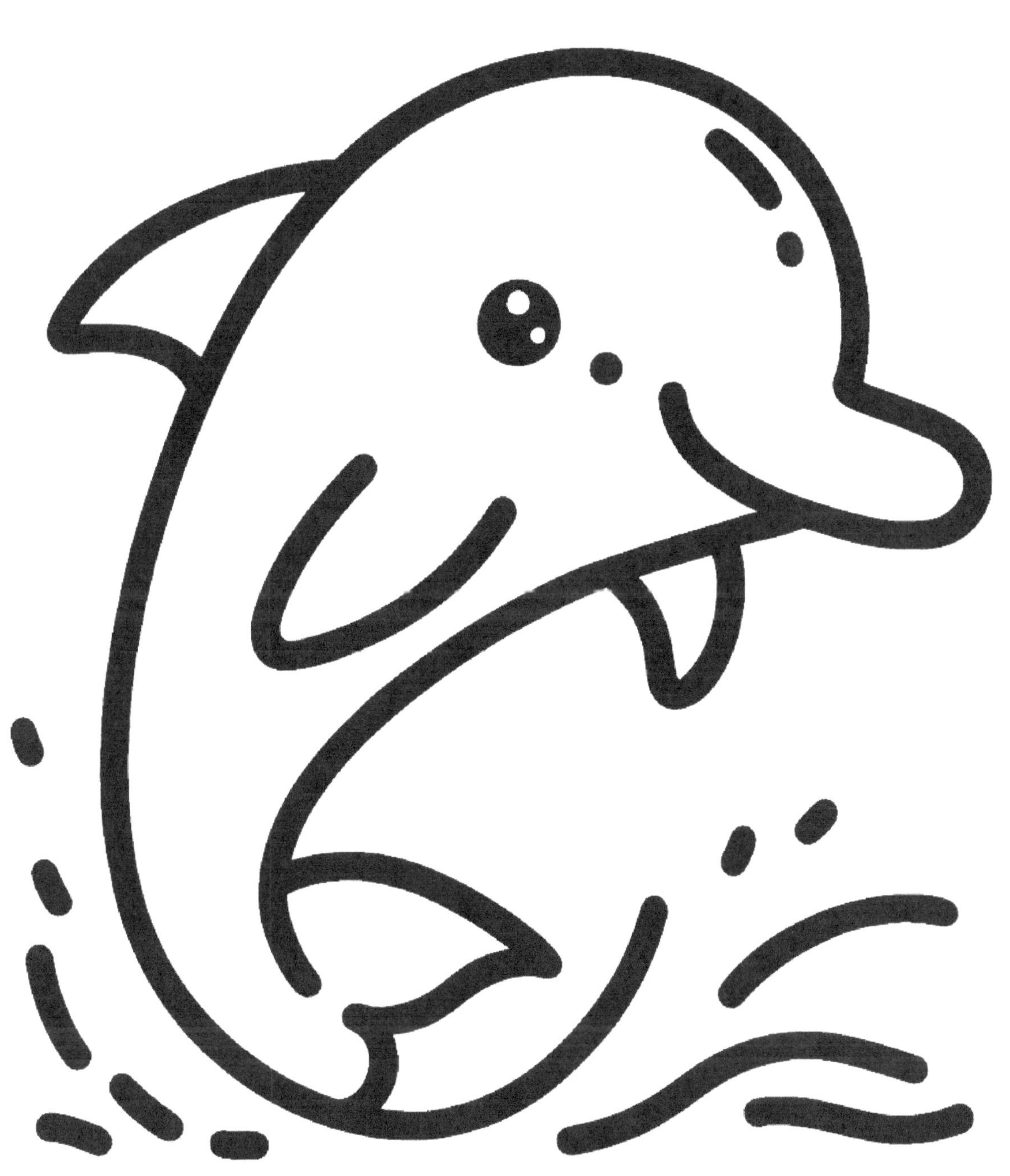

ALLIGATOR

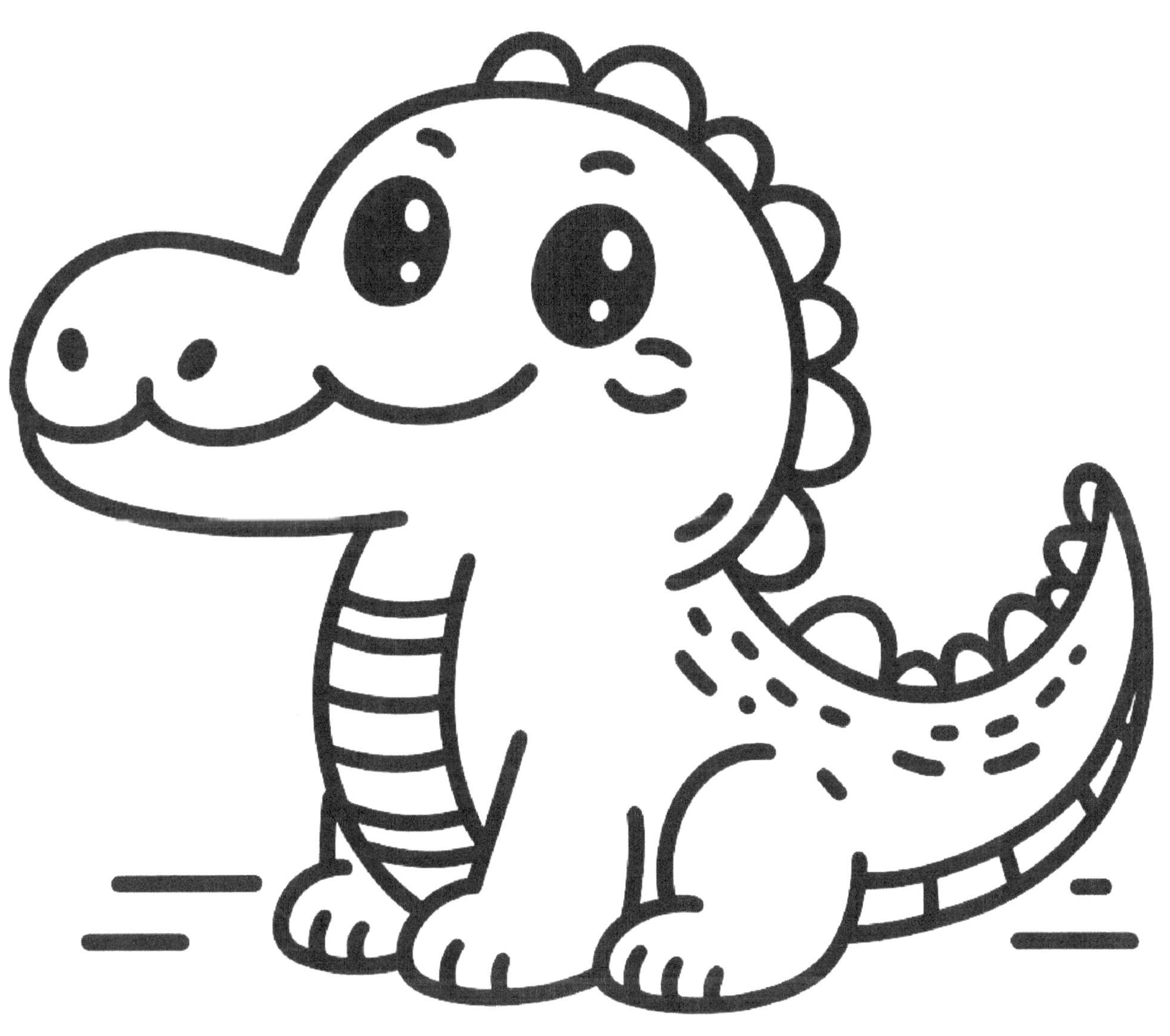

RHINOCEROS

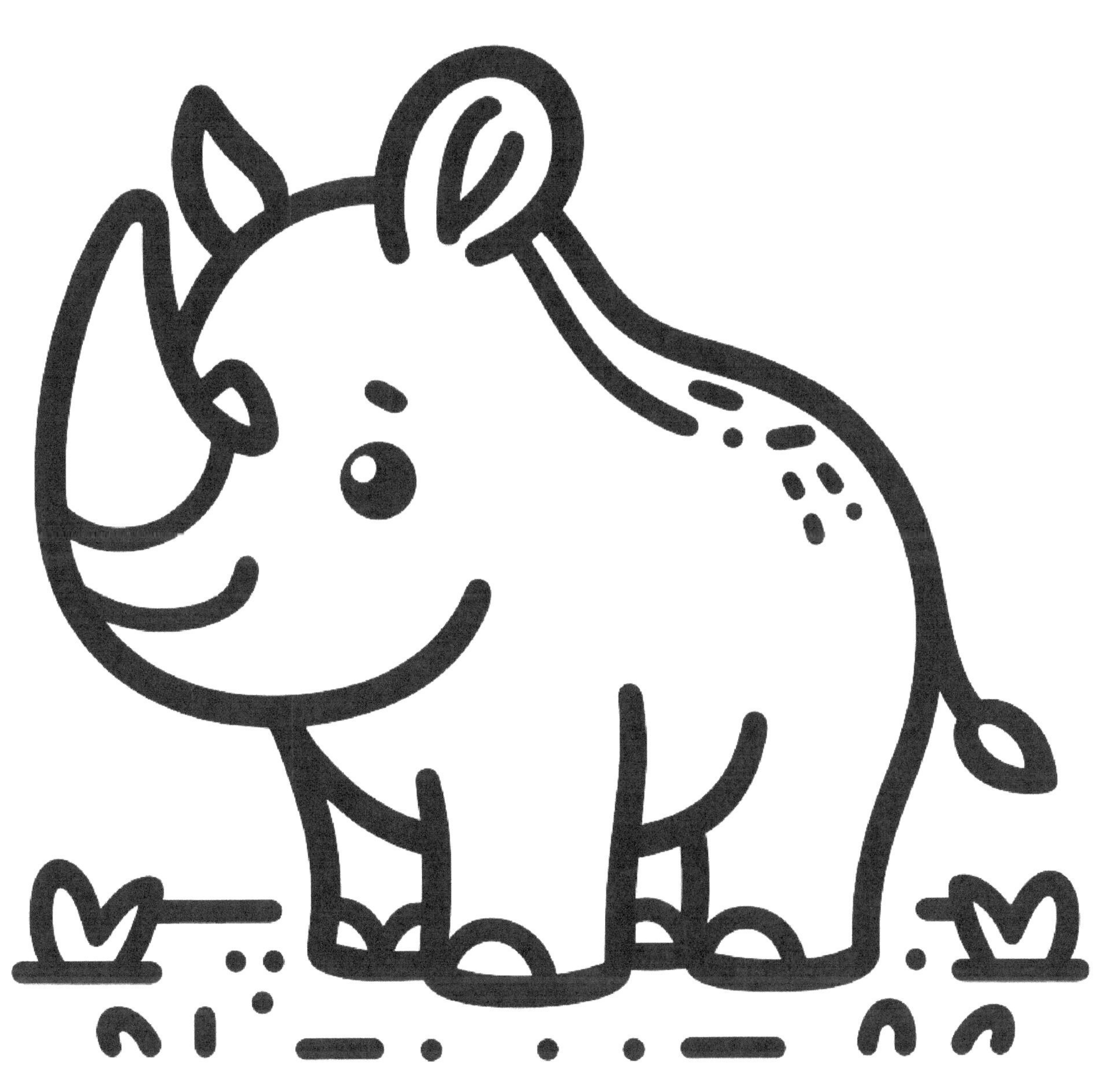

ZEBRA

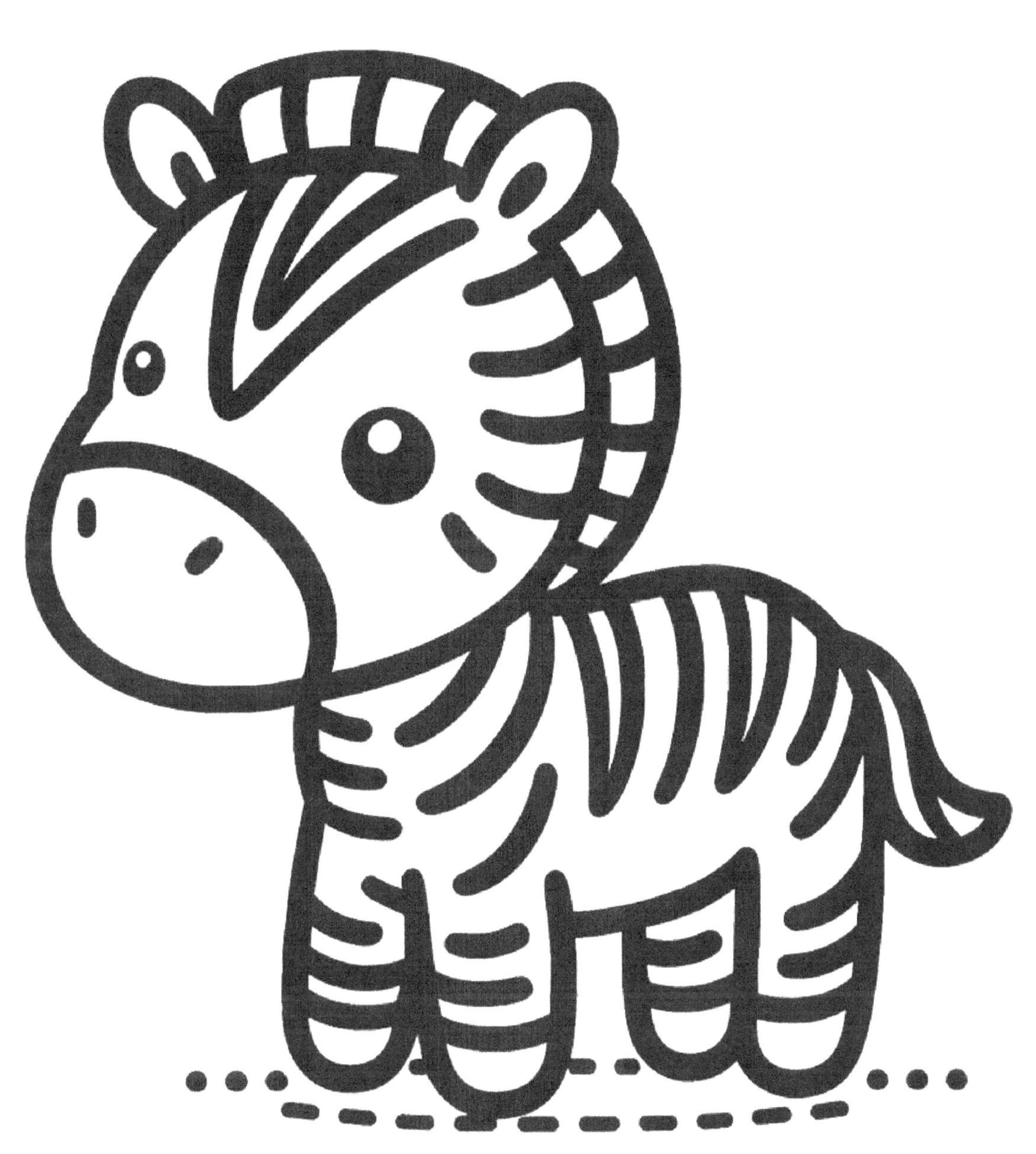

PARROT

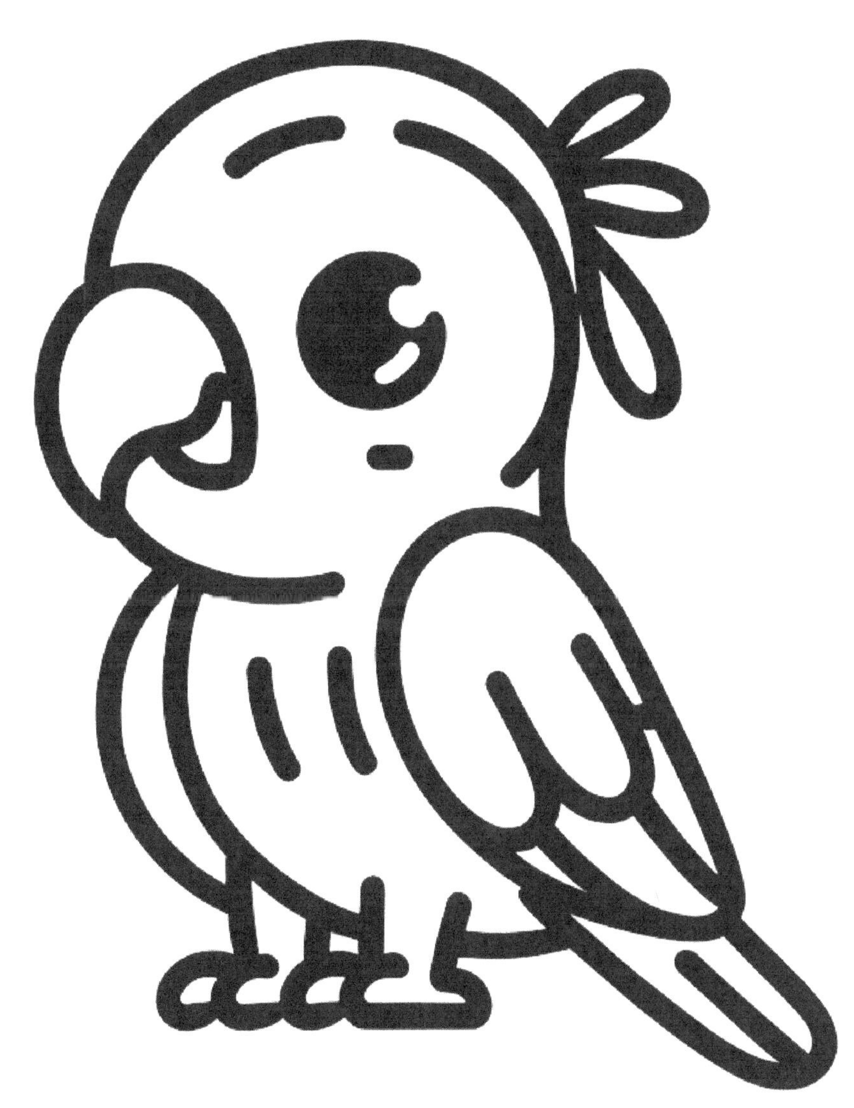

HIPPOPOTAMUS

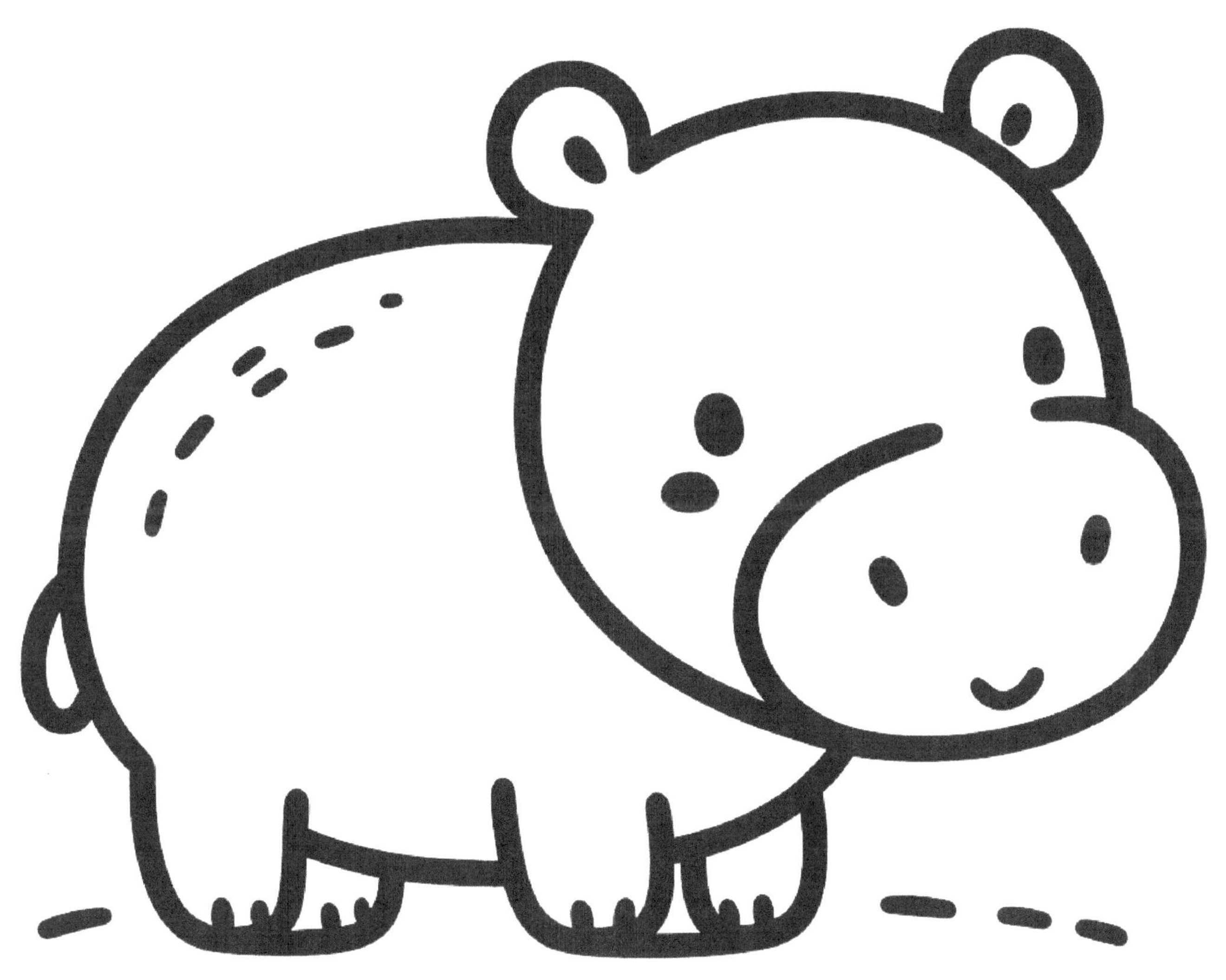

MONKEY

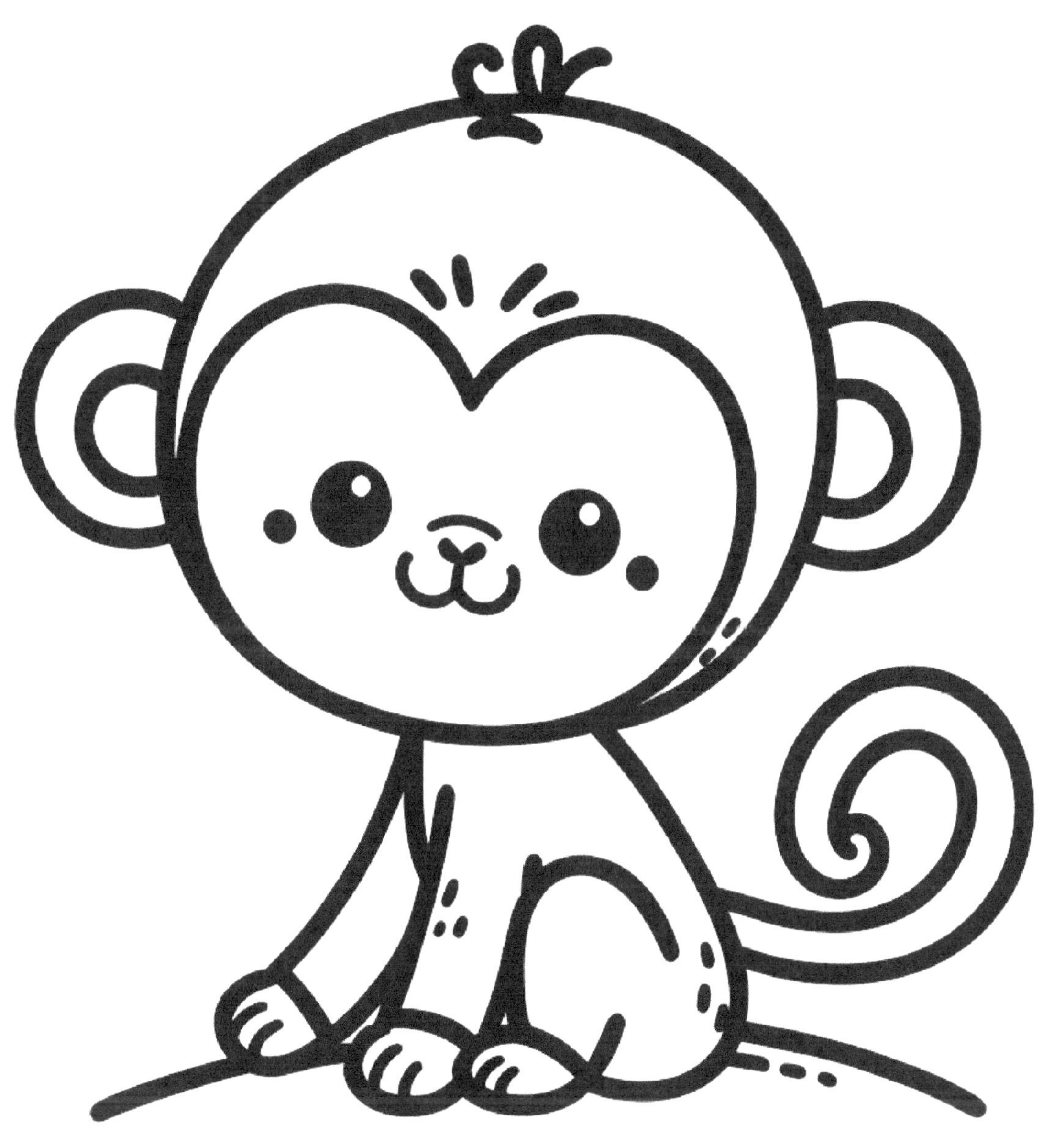

PEACOCK

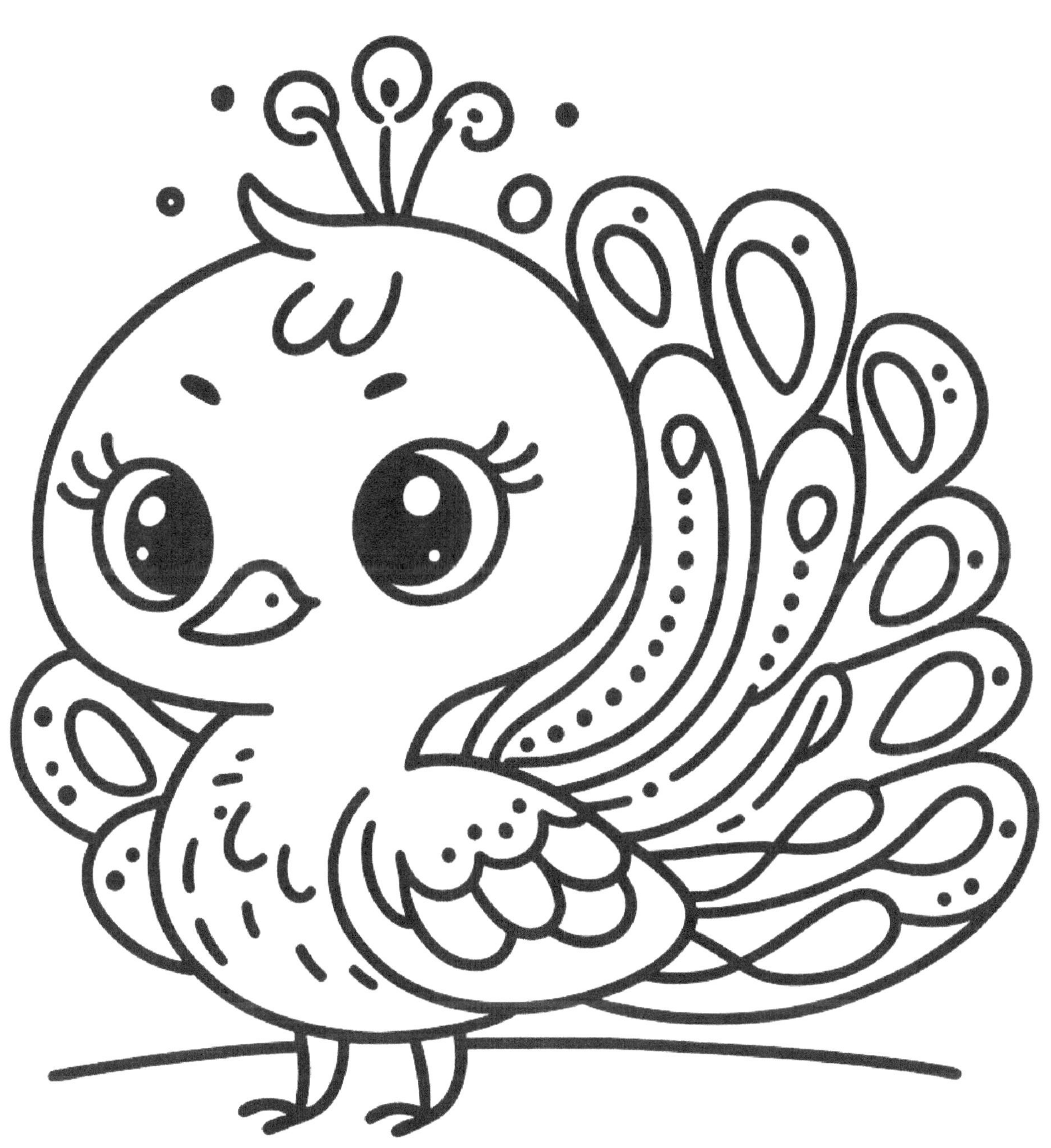

KANGAROO

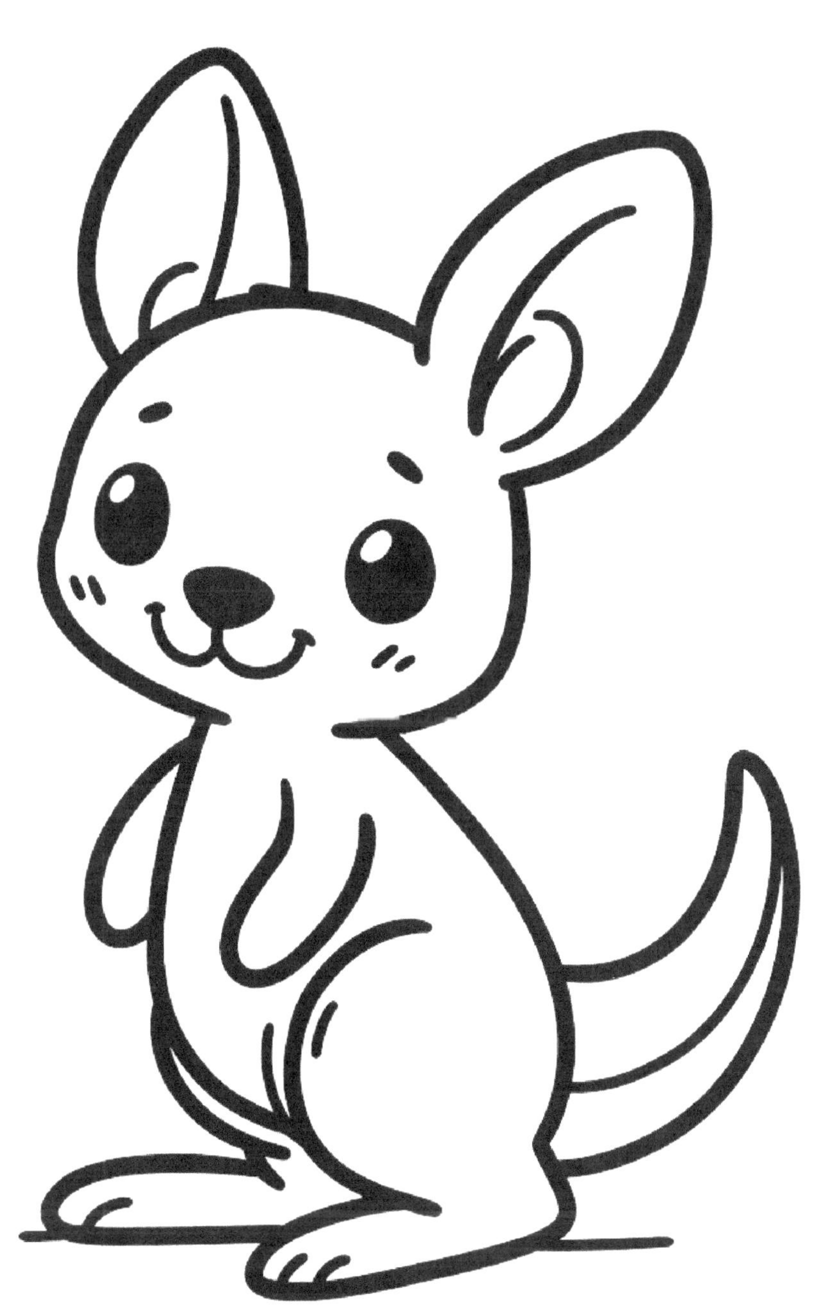

CAMEL

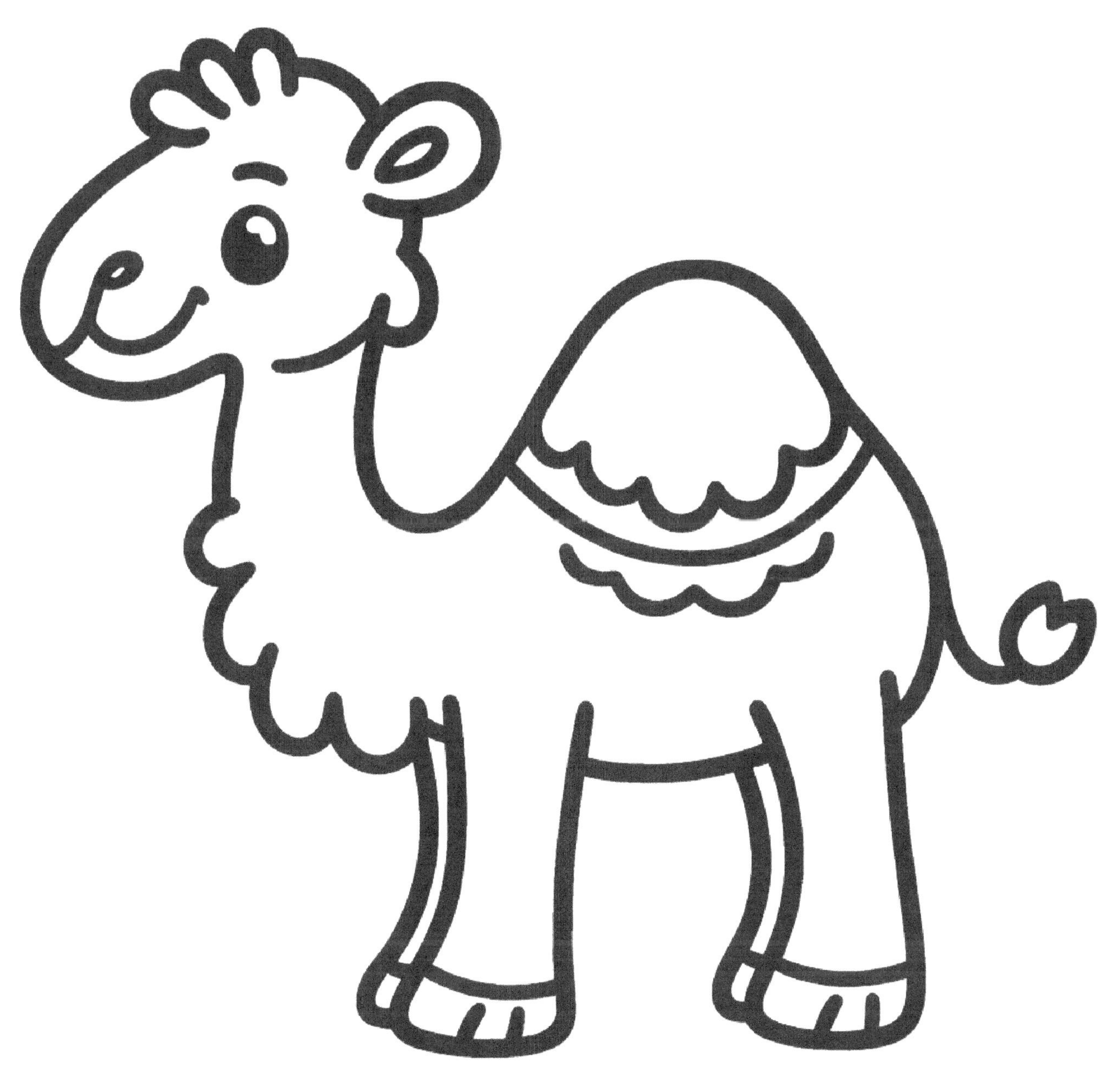

OWL

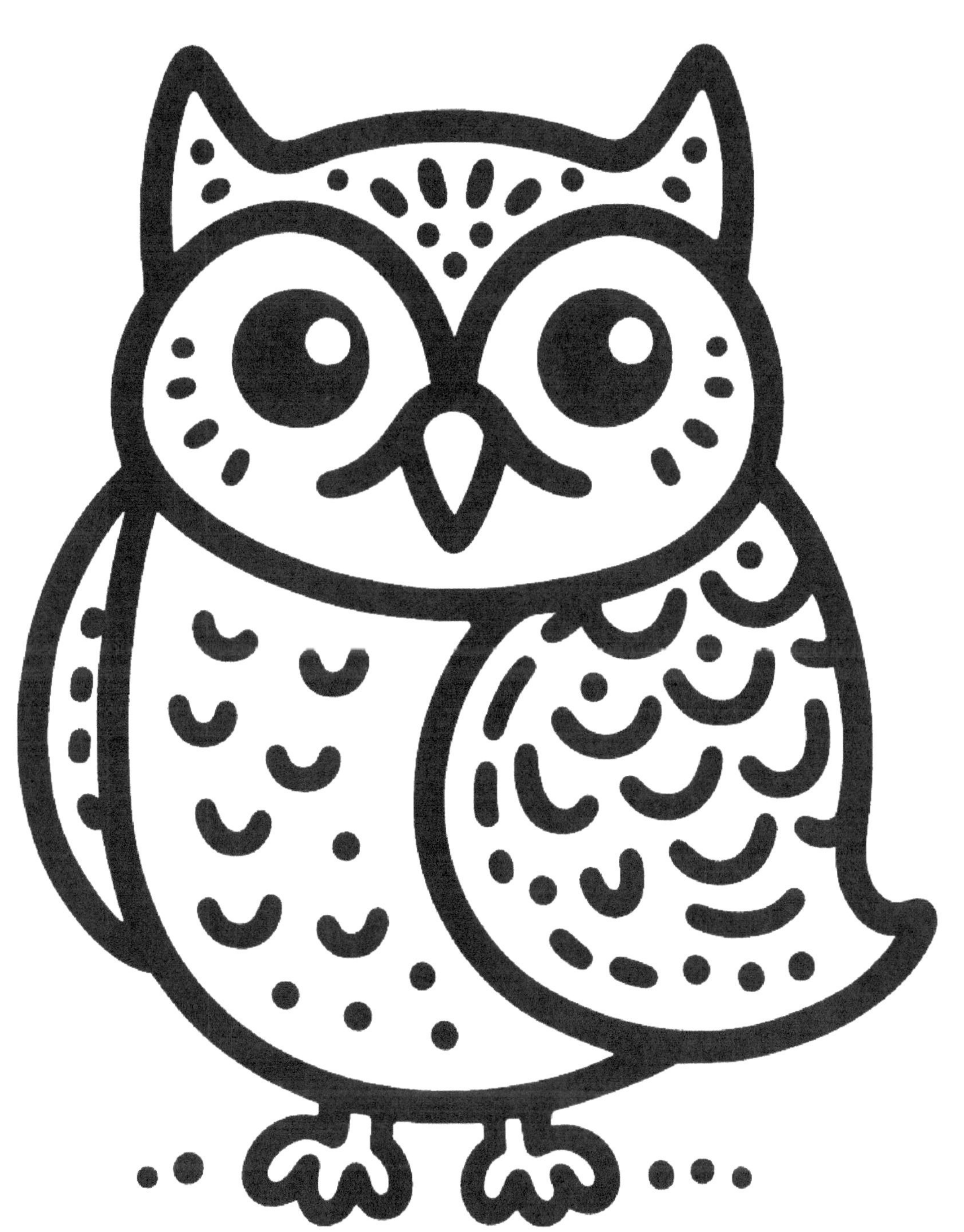

RABBIT

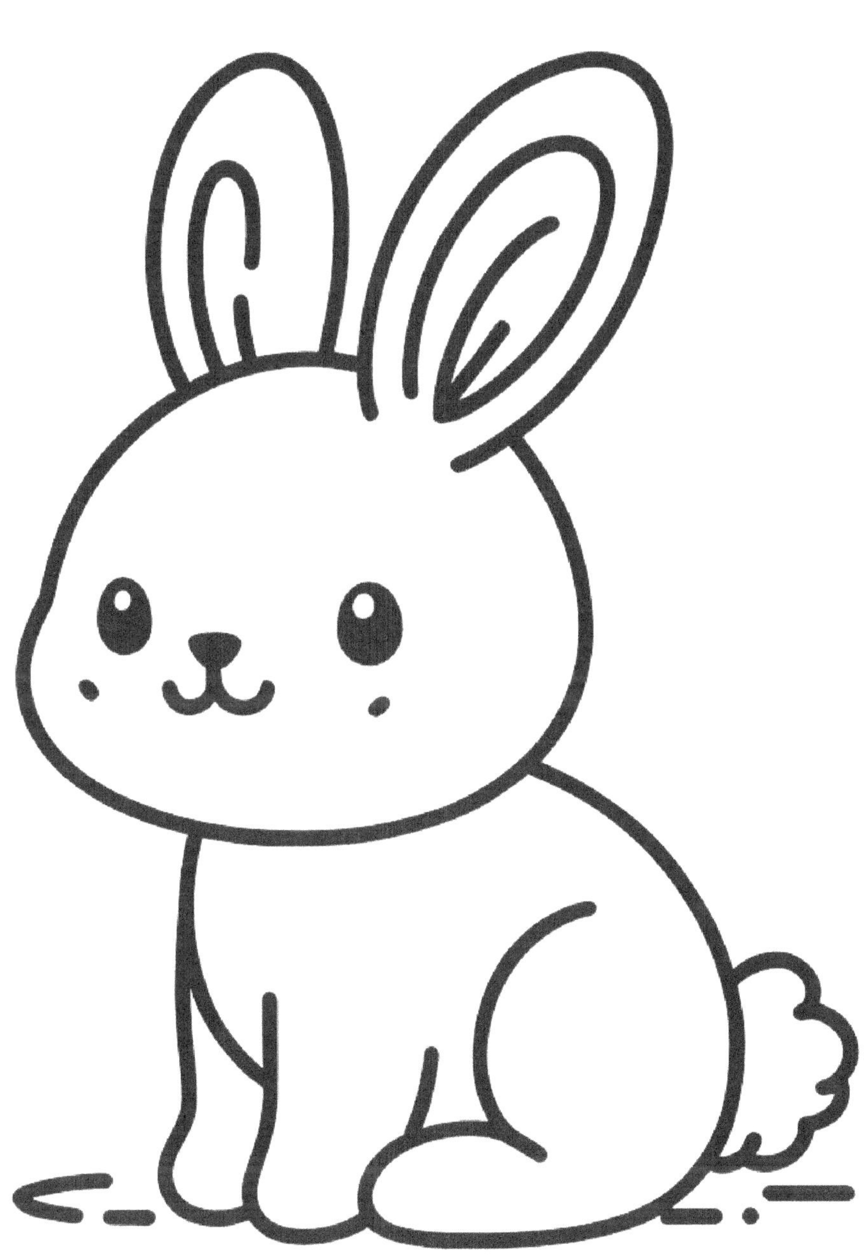

FOX

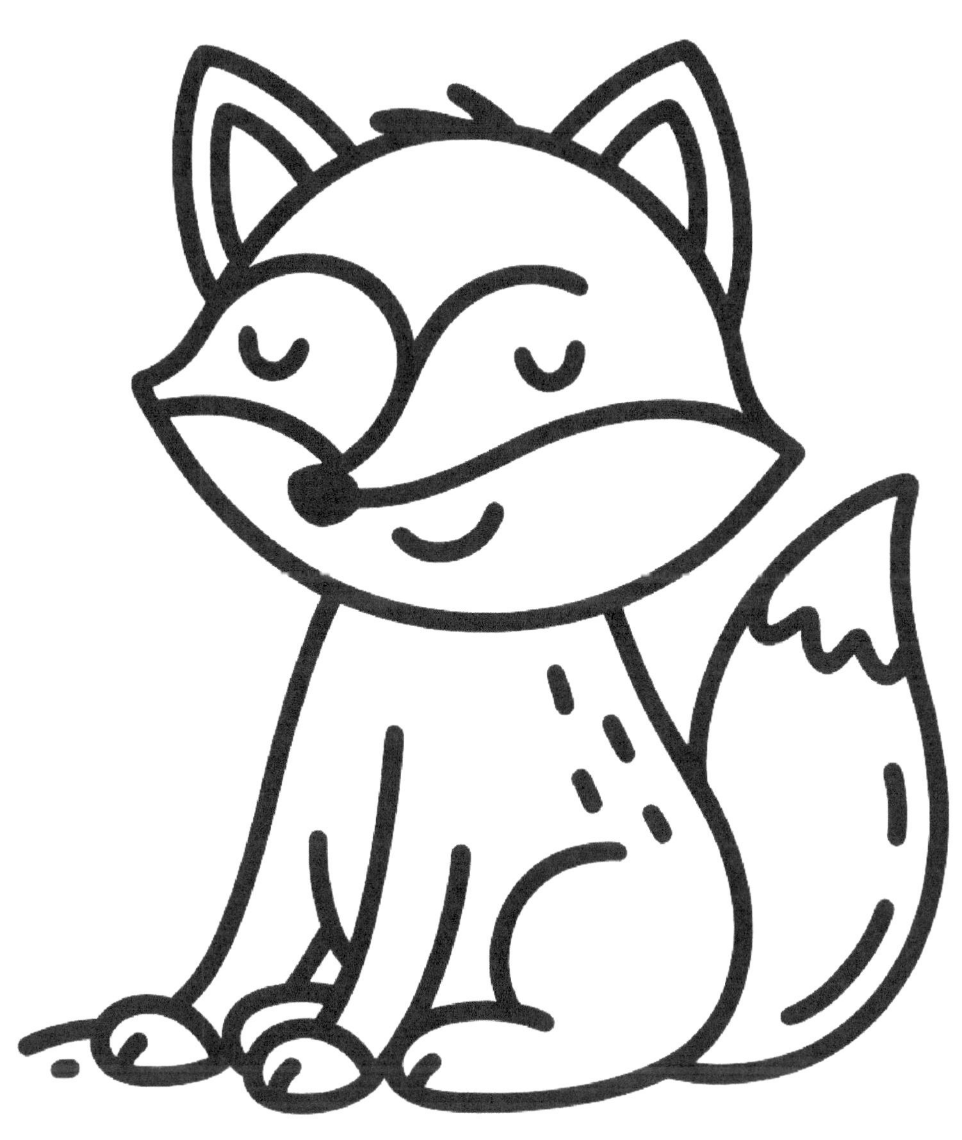

DEER

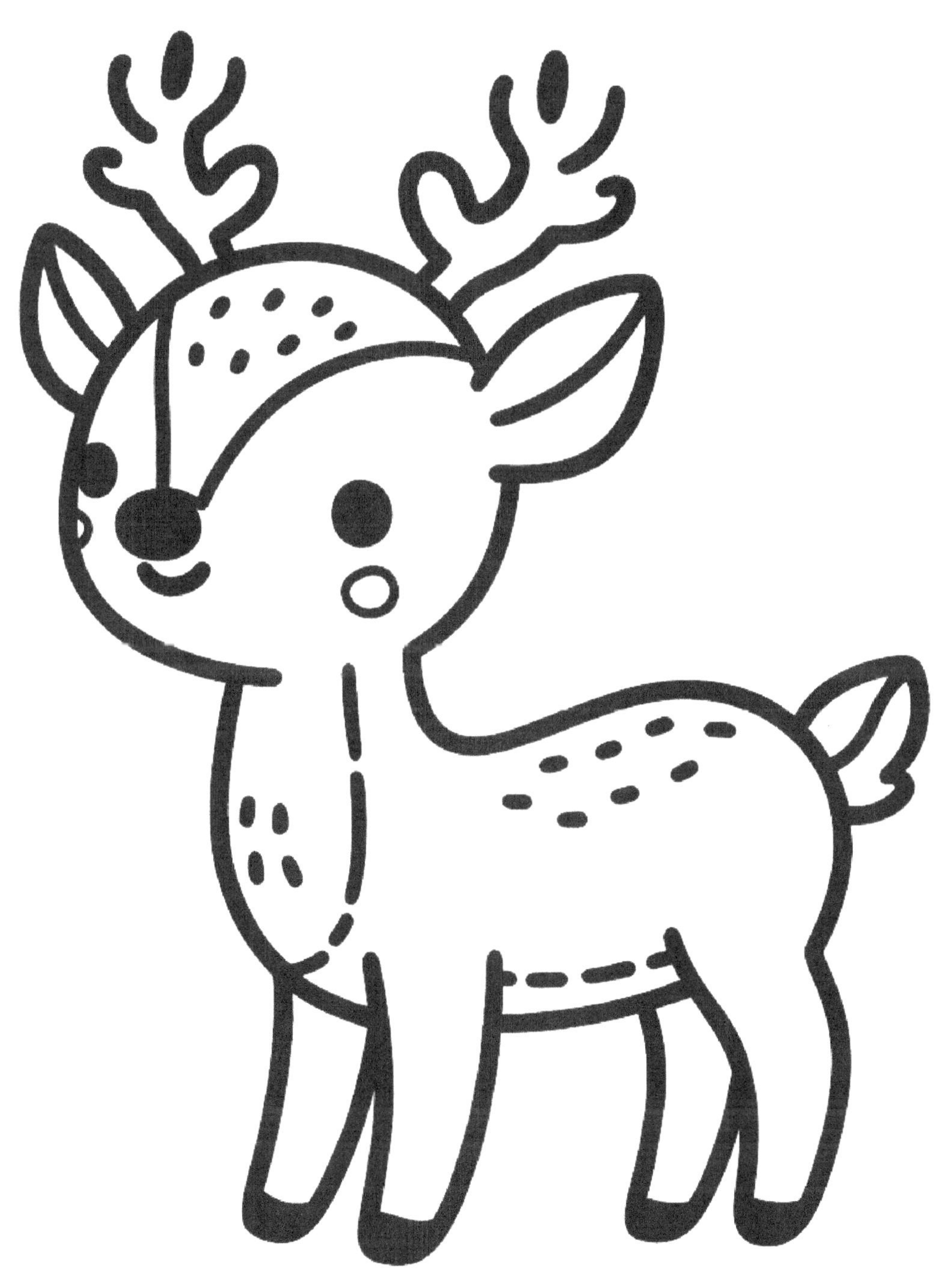

TURTLE